an emotional

KALEIDOSCOPE

c.m. sullivan

an emotional kaleidoscope

a short collection of poems

This collection features fictional and nonfictional events, feelings, and thoughts.

Printed in the United States of America

First Printing: 2019

ISBN: 978-1-64516-047-2

IngramSpark Publishing

Cover Art: Robin Vuchnich

For those who didn't wish upon a star.

For those who said "never," to a dream.

For Corky, one of the first people who truly believed in my dream and who continues to believe in my dreams. Thank you for always being my flashlight.

For my family, who has been there since day one.

And for Barb and Christy, the two most veracious supporters a young writer and future teacher could have under their wings. I love you both—always. Thank you both so much for being the radiant rainbows that you are.

*"We are a kaleidoscope of complicated intricacies.
A million different facets of light and darkness."*

— K. M. Keeton

contents

---

foreword

c.m. sullivan's debut collection of poems, *an emotional kaleidoscope*, focuses on the fluidity of life, and the cascading emotions inherent in living a complex, rich, and full existence. Sullivan's poetry celebrates of the entirety of life. The collection, as a whole, is a deeply meditative observance of suffering, acceptance, love of self and others, and exquisite joy. Sullivan makes clear that the journey of becoming—who we are, as close to our true selves as possible—is a journey worth taking. The process of self-realization, acceptance, and love leads to a more authentic appreciation of all of the colors, all of the intricate shades on our emotional spectrum.

In vivid imagery, sensuous language, imaginative form, and diction that leaps musically off the page (or whispers intimately in the reader's ear, or bluntly expresses pain), these poems are painted richly on the canvas of each page. Individually they stand-alone strong, but their accumulative effect reflects the journeying we must do, again and again, to know, accept and love our individual selves and others. The most satisfying experience a teacher can have is to learn from her students. Here, Sullivan has taught me about the tightrope of inspiration and discipline. He's walked, high above the crowd, and created an emotional experience I won't soon forget. He's spoken to my own process of becoming, and how all of us must reimagine ourselves and our lives at some point, and honestly, often more than once.

This collection holds what we, as readers know to be true—we cannot grasp or fix a single emotional experience. Emotions are like quick silver, mercurial, and our job is to be present, at full attention, fully inhabiting the moments and experiences that bead together into our lives, whether they lead to rejoicing or humble us to our knees. I will say this reading experience was a singularly joyful one. c.m. sullivan, once my student, and now my teacher.

— Barbara C. Lawhorn

dear friend,

Emotions consume all of our being. It takes all of our efforts to not let the bulk of their impact crush us and to keep on keeping on, even through the pain.

We live each day through our emotions—they are the core of our being. Emotions get us through the hard times and help us appreciate the good. They ground us, so we don't fly away from even ourselves. Without emotions, we wouldn't truly live.

The poems you're about to consume come from a scattered mind that tried its hardest to string ideas together collectively. I hope you find them in the same light that I did. Each has helped me to evolve from a past emotion that I feared I'd never escape (yes, even the happiest of emotions!). Highlight words, verses, stanzas that you resonate with you. Write in the margins with *your* memories and connections. Cry if you need a good cry, smile if you need a smile. I strived to make my experiences relatable to each reader by dividing them into several factions of emotion—find what suits your experiences and mindsets and run wild.

Writing has truly helped me and I so encourage you—yes, you holding this paperback or e-book—to give writing a shot. It helped me dump the feelings and thoughts that were clogging my brain onto the page or my Word document. Pick up a cheap journal and an ink pen and write for ten minutes a day. See if you see improvements in your mindset. Even if you feel like you aren't a "good writer," try it. You decide who reads your thoughts.

Writing has taught me to be honest with myself and what I'm feeling and what I'm thinking about certain instances. It forces you to get everything out once you get the ball rolling in the ink pen. It clears your mind and helps you sleep better, with your worries etched in your journal. Writing each day has truly helped me see that I *can* conquer even the scariest of fears.

While I was in the writing process for this book, I was taken aback by the mere range of human emotion. We are capable of feeling so many emotions—from fear to sadness to joy to surprise to anticipation to disappointment to ecstatic bliss to contentment to anger to hatred to udder happiness—I found that I was drawn to the darker emotions most. Not that I feel I am a negative, but just we remember the feeling of the most painful of emotions. For example, you'll always remember the feeling of your first heartbreak or the first time you were let down or when you beyond pissed off—you'll forever be able to recall those dark, dark feelings. Furthermore, I noticed the poems I wrote more easily were the darker emotions: self-loathing, sadness, heartbreak. And that I had to really push myself and think harder to write the "lighter" emotions: peace, love (although love at this point is easily a cliché), and liberation.

As you go through each section, acknowledge that to feel authentic love, you must experience a painful heartbreak first to show you what you truly deserve. And to feel confident or liberated, you must hit the lowest of lows at least once in your life to make the highest so high. These challenges and hurdles are what test us and push us to grow. Once you've become accustomed to the balance of human emotions, you can truly experience a *kaleidoscope* of emotions.

–c.m. sullivan

self-loathing + anxiety

i am searching
for all that
i lost

i am reaching
for all that
i wished for

i am falling short
on all those
dreams i once dreamed

i am searching
for the
person i've yet to become

- *identity*

i wish i
didn't wish for things i
can't obtain

-   *be careful what you're wishing for*

dammit, doubt!

I feel as though I hate
myself today—and for that
I say, "dammit, doubt!"

i chase
all of the things
i push—
away

-    *self-realization*

anxiety's haiku

You couldn't sleep be—
—cause you kept thinking you were—
—n't good enough, too.

You laid there in the
darkness unraveling and
couldn't stop yourself.

In the morning hours,
the sun woke your fears by shin—
—ing a light on them.

It takes time, they say—
which it's true!—Don't forget to
breathe and smile and laugh.

you and i,
we are different—
not the same—
two parts that
don't equal one

i hate that i
am not
like you

-    *when you compare yourself to others*

semicolon

I am a semicolon—

Defined as a pause between two innate clauses
        —I am a semicolon.

I am neither there nor here,
        —I am a semicolon.

I can't be in or out,
        —I am a semicolon.

I don't belong with you or her,
        —I am a semicolon.

I never feel hot or cold,
        —I am a semicolon.

I don't belong at all;
        therefore, I am nothing but a misused semicolon—

i could be many things,
yes, i could—
but all i wanted to was to fit in

-     *determined to be damned*

somebody i once knew

stranger,

i'm staring into your dark, shadowy eyes and it's like i'm staring into your soul. and the scary part—i can't escape it. i've been captured and locked in a dungeon cell beneath the earth where there's an absence of light. *help me,* i cried out, but turned over no relief, no rescue. i was alone and i was scared and i didn't know who you were at the time. i didn't know what to do or what to say to make the hurt hurt less or make the unknown known. i was just *there.* i wasn't receptive to pain—the definition slipped my mind in your presence—i was okay with bleeding, with crying, with hurting, with wanting you to do the worst so that i could just feel *something, anything, everything.* you bruised me, you burnt me and i hold onto these scars, cuts, slashes, burns, and blisters because for the first time in my life, i feel something inside me that's *real.* it's a foreign entity in my body, a feeling—a *being*—i've never welcomed in to stay, but i think this time i will for it isn't so bad after all, these feelings. i feel comfortable and stable and everything my therapist says i'm not and everything she says i shouldn't be feeling isn't what i should be feeling, but i like it and i want it to stick. i want to stay. i never want it to leave. these feelings get me. they know me, truly know me—why would i dare kick them out like an unwanted guest when they're the ones who've been there in my mind from the start like a relative? i've tried, in life, far too long to feel the same way as everyone else—and it's been a great run while it lasted—but every age comes to an end, every good character eventually dies off. this is that shedding, and stranger, i have you to thank. stranger, you've shown me it's not so lonely to feel alone and it's not so bad to feel so sad. i embrace even these feelings for they are the ones i'll look back upon and say *remember when* once i've found my way.

thank you, stranger.

sincerely,
just some outsider

endless, sleepless nights

a darkened room, you sit in and wonder
what led you here—to this state
and why had He given you this to think.
answers go unanswered most nights;
yet, still you wonder at night
those same damn questions you wish
someone—if *anyone*—could, would, should
answer.

foggy glass

I cannot see through the Foggy Glass.
Its misty wall—how wonderful and wary—welcomes me
to see inside, but I can't.
All I wish is to see—

the Future remains untold—
and I still strive for its answers,
to break out of this Murderous Mold—
and finally, see what Life has written for me

haunted

at night, i scream in my sleep and sweat through my sheets. it's never a restful night, it's always something. there's always something lurking behind you, just waiting, waiting to trip you and knock you down. it will try to knock you down. and, sadly, i'm okay with that. i let it knock me down, not because of the pain, but of what pain stands for. for the fact that in that instance of being shoved down, i feel something—no, not just *something*—something *real*. the idea of feeling something real excites me, it motivates me, it tells me that there's still a life worth living. so i appreciate those things that haunt my nighttime brain, my darkened room, my barren pit of a stomach from skipping out on meals i knew i should've eaten, but spit out in the bathroom in shame. this feeling of pain keeps me grounded, it keeps in the thundering bellies of life because of its realness and it's so real it has its own name and i hate myself more because i don't know its name. i feel so much shame for not knowing its name; yet, i fear this fact the most for i never have known its name and probably never will.

"You'll never have that body."
Pulls at flab of flesh,
and thinks to self—
*Why did God put me in this
bleak body?*

-      *self-image*

perception

in the innermost crevice of my heart,
i hold this statement true and evergreen:
i know i'll get there, but i'm just not there

        yet.

i can't shake it, for it's true that i know
the innate interworking of the journey;
the stage is set for the actor to take his bow,
and i applaud.
the props are placed for act ii, scene ii, but the
show's just begun and i'm antsy in my seat
ready for the action to wreck down the walls
of others, so that i may feel at ease
within my own sense of being.
production's wrapped and we're out in the lobby
greeting women and men of other bodies.
to start is to finish, to breathe is to live; for,
we all feel the pouring reign of emotions—anxious,
depressed, uncertainty, impatience—nay, they try to trip
us, knock us down, make us bleed, bleed blood red.
Oh, skinn'd th' knee of me to see that i'm merely mortal
flesh in this perceived rack of godly bones.
it's disreputable, really, how i'd not acknowledged such
       truth planted side-by-side, row-by-row of corn
       stalks rooted in the black, rich soil of other people's
       shit.

life on the outside

Join the team—
            —chase the dream
and fly with the greats—

Go big and loud—
            —fight for what you believe
and do so indefinitely 'til the end—

Imagine a lifetime—
            —one so grand, you burst
and one that makes even skeptics shiver—

Ask yourself *how can we reach that*
            —when all else fails
and dreams go unanswered; promises broken

To dream is to believe
            —and to fight to live,
but those who can't—won't—

sadness + heartbreak

i was dripping with sadness
the day you came into my life—
you brought me foreign fantasies;
happy for a moment, broken the next—
i was drenched with tears
the day you walked out of my life—
you left me with detectible disappointment—
broken then, broken now

- *bleeding hearts*

fucking liar

i spent so much time on you for you to spend yours on someone else. you'd tell me things to reassure things between us. things like *i wish we could make it work,* but then you contradict yourself by avoiding, ignoring, blocking me. you said things like *let me buy you a dinner you won't forget and take you out to a movie you've been dying to see,* then i don't hear from you for weeks. so how should i interpret it when you say i'm cute and sweet and smart and everything you're looking for

                              but
                                   you
                                        walk
                                             away
                                        from
                                   me
                              every
                         damn
                    time.
               you're
          nothing
     but
          a
               fucking
                    liar
                         and
                              i
                                   never
                                        want
                         to
                              see
                         you
                    again.

cold bath water

without a doubt, this wasn't ideal
i never imagined we'd be here,
but life throws curveballs
every now and then to keep it fresh.

on the first date, you seemed genuinely interested
and that it *might* work—
but nothing affirmative, though—
that'd be too much for you
to rattle around in your twisted, pathetic head
and don't lie, you know it's true.

our conversations were buried
sometime last week,
the corpse is still cold to the touch.
things haven't had time to settle
or break down—except my heart, of course.
it's always my fucking heart.

and i hate myself for writing
and thinking
and dreaming
and singing
and wondering
about you—
i know deep down
you ~~don't~~ will never deserve
my heart
my love
my soul
my thoughts

my anything—
like our communication,
you're dead to me.

ice cream boy

9:34pm
i head your way in the dark,
i don't care that it's so late,
once i get there, see you, it'll all be great.

10:49pm
i can't get over how fuckin adorable
you are—more so in person, dammit, *kiss me.*

11:47pm
i'm crashin into your waves
breathin in the salty waters, chokin, drownin.

12:14am
goodbye will come,
but i don't want to go.

12:28am
i'll remember this night forever
and ever and ever, because it's the night
that i jumped all in, off the cliff
and still lived.

12:55am
dropped you off,
against my will.

1:37am
i sent you a snap thankin you for the night,
but you hit me back with a playful diss—
it was then that i knew i wouldn't see you again.

1:38am
fuck you, ice cream boy.

yet

I want to cry and scream,
       yet nothing escapes my mouth.

I want to kick and flail my arms,
       yet I remain motionless in a sea of anger.

I fight to bite my tongue for all the times I wished I spoke,
       yet didn't.

I courageously curse out loud for all the consecutive failures,
       yet I don't feel remorse.

I try to remind myself that there's always a reason for everything,
       yet it still feels as though I should give up trying.

And yet, and yet, and yet again I breathe in
       and out, yet it still fucking burns.

They tell me to keep breathing,
       yet all I want to—

And I can't—I can't breathe when each time it stings even more,
       yet they tell me to "man up," and to "move on."

I conform to their demands when all else fails even when I don't
understand the brutality behind my own actions,

       yet I do it anyway.

hand in the mouth of the flame

i never learn, do i?
the flame draws me in
the delicacy of its dance
captures my attention and it's all
i can do to not reach out and touch it

i touch it

i've touched it
and now i'm burnt,
like i didn't know that'd happen
i keep putting my hand in the fire
only to keep getting burnt out on love

can we go back to the summer of 2009?

simpler times, indeed—
what happened to your life?
decade later, you're lost
in your own damn reflection.
who the hell am are you anyway?
each day you feel like a carbon copy,
not as good as the original.

life was easier
when you had disney channel
coming through the tv at 7:00
to watch the latest sitcom
that you didn't dare to ditch
out on.

fast forward 120 months—
you are stumbling down the stairs,
not only wondering where you are,
but where the hell you're going
to end once (if) you reach the finish line.

distance between

we're kinda in a pickle:

you and i are
practically perfect
when paired side by side,

but it sucks that our
souls and hearts
can't ever be conjoined

you say i'm great,
but i think you're great,
and then you say it just can't work.

so i'm not hiding the hurt
when you text or snap
me, i secretly still wish

there wasn't so much
distance between

us

ghost of you

dearest dear—
i swore i smelled your scent
last night in my closet.
i laid in bed thinking—too hard—
about how your aftershave linger'd
and float'd up my nose. the weight
of your pungent, pine-scented cologne.

damn you—
i *know* i saw a shift in the room,
a shape of you in the darken'd distance.
you were there; or at least,
a ghost of you.

salty-sweetness—
were you there?
was it my too creative-imagination
clogging up the machine again?
am i dreaming up some crazy concoction
that's nothing more than a haunted love-sick dream?

please let me know.

love,

the one you used to love.

permanent marker

I draw on my skin with a permanent marker,
the grooves hug onto the rich black ink.
I try to rub it, rub it off, but it only gets darker.
"*Dammit*! I'm stained," I think.
My mind lingers in that instance for the worse,
will I ever become untainted again?
My body feels heavy and stiff as a corpse.
And as I lay here, I stare and stare at the stain,
telling myself it won't ever wash off.
Idiot — I've drawn as if I didn't assume it'd stick
forever. I emerge the abstract canvas in a water-filled trough,
    scrubbing mercilessly. Nothing — not a budge.
    Words hold the same weight; careful not too much.

can't wait to meet you, you said once
you're so cute, you said once
cutie and sweet talker, you called me once

-     lies i believed for far too long

boys only burn
bridges that could've been golden
they tear at our hearts
and toy with our minds
leaving us stranded
on an island of mixed emotions

- *boys ~~can~~ suck ~~sometimes~~ all the time*

walmart parking lot

everything's fine and i'm not crying, you're crying
and if one of us isn't it, why do we keep on trying?
we are two lincoln logs being repeatedly jammed
into a slot too small to fit right. we need to give up while
we're winning, but are we really winning if we're crying?

sad music blasting, speakers breaking at each rattle of the beat
i can't help but look to my right and cry more at the empty seat.
you were always the taylor swift song waiting to be written
by me and i put it off for far too long simply because it was
too delicate to touch. sadly, it hurts because i knew you all too well.

don't tell me to stop coming here late at night, it's our spot
regardless of a relationship, connection—this is our parking lot.
i come here often and sit in the vacant memories still warm to the
touch. i'm stupid and crazy in love with the idea of being with you.
even though you're out of price range, i'd drop every dollar i had
for you
        and it still wasn't enough for you.
        i hate that i love you still,
        but you're still you,
        and i still love those
        midnight kisses still lingering
        through the air of walmart's parking lot

wrecked and slowly sinking

Broke my heart it did in two
his name it left your mouth—
Torn your picture from my wall I did
to keep my heart—what's left—intact.
Honesty, though, I admire—
aches, that truth it causes.
I tell myself I'll never love but again—
for you wrecked me that day you did so wrong—

i can't wait to fill my journal with thoughts of you
i can't wait to tell my journal the moments shared with you
how you stole my heart
the same day
you stabbed it—
killing my belief in love.
i can't wait to cry my eyes out tonight at the memory of you.

- *when i fell, i fell a part*

i can't keep up with boys like you;
one day, i'm *cute*
the next, i'm ignored

then—
i'm alone.

-    *confused as fuck*

but i do

Not all feel as lost as I
    —but I do enjoy the feeling

Not all feel love as I
    —but I do fall hopelessly often

Not all wonder about those things as I
    —but I do strive for the striking suspense

Not all who dream believe
    —but I do imagine a world as such

    I do see, with my feeble eye,
    a world worth conceiving—
    But I do picture, clear as day,
    a life worth living for—

daffodils + teardrops

The Flowers in the Murky Water have long ago died—
you've lived each day in your room, and have painstakingly Cried
yourself to sleep each night. She brought a vase—
of Daffoldils last month for you to regain your place
in her heart. Your Tears have since ceased and dried—
and you're breathing once again, not yet standing tall with pride.
Why go after Happiness when it shall only chase
you in the end? How can we withstand the hourglass of time and
grace—
In Heaven and Hell, we all go there hereafter, for one of the Two to
Take—
and as we say our final Good-byes, our hearts endure a celestial
Break—

you told me about your past
and to me, i assumed you promised me your future

-   *unintentional lies*

i remembered you like a childhood memory
and cried
and cried
and cried
until
i

couldn't

stop

-    *torrential downpour*

boys be stupid

Boys be stupid, yes they do—
excuses—I didn't ask but none—

Break hearts they do so often—
yes, it's true, boys be stupid.

Liars and cheaters—
boys—stupid they are!

Trust 'em—we cannot
all of our secrets they'll break.

Love 'em for what they are—stupid—
but fight to keep the time we'd let 'em waste.

Boys be stupid—it's been proven,
no lie—boys: stupid they are.

i
hate—*hate*
that
you
fill
up
my
thoughts
with
dreams
that
won't
come
true

the radio plays your song today
and i think about your voice cracking
as you tried to belt out each chorus.
i turn it off in a heartbeat
and i wipe the tear slowly sliding down
my hot, rosy cheeks
and drive home in still silence.

-    *your song still haunts me*

i deleted your pic
faster than you
depleted my heart

- *this one's for you, douchebag #7*

plucking petals

he loves me,
he loves me not.
he loves me,
he loves me not.
when i stop,
this time,
my wish will
come true.
he loves me
he loves me—

    not.

love's quite the funny thing, it is—
i twirl at the thought of what you're doing
that it fucks with what i'm doing.
it feels like i'm cheating, when it fucks me
that i'm with someone new, someone
who actually cares for me and me for me

-    *self-pleasure*

you were a fairy tale
        i told myself
                to believe

                    in love
                      again

my car still smells of your aftershave
and every time i take a drive, i daydream
of you driving back to me

-   *driving while daydreaming*

thank you for being a dick

thank you for everything—
from the lessons learned about understanding my dignity,
what i stand for, what i put up with, and what i act upon—
thank you for everything.

no joke—i'm fortunate for the shitty experience.
you taught me that i need to look harder,
lower my expectations, not my standards;
muchas gracias, mi amor

please quit actin like you 'did me dirty,'
i'm not the one with problems knowin what i want
and what i don't. if anything,
i'm honestly sorry that you had to make yourself
look like an ass as you
destroyed my serenity
because you've yet
to discover your own sexual identity.

venomous

love's a snake you don't see in the grass
you step on it unaware
of its teeth and venom
slipping into your bloodstream

love's a snake you don't see in the grass
it hisses and snaps and slithers away
all too quickly to address that
something sizzling in your bloodstream

love's a snake you don't see in the grass
with fangs sharp as its blunt personality
it always, always ends so sour—with a
searing so severe in your bloodstream

daisy dreams

I imagine a love that only can live in a dream;

he who walks so veraciously that my heart sways to his beat
he who sweet talks me into a candy-like bliss
he who encompasses all of my thoughts, like a thief, he steals my
mind—
    my mind it wonders to all the things i want to do with him,

    but don't

i **desire** a love that only burns those it touches;

a love that is saturated in each hue of the rainbow, so bright, so
vibrant i'm blinded
a love that is luring me in to a trance i can't ever escape
a love that is simple and kind and sticky and everything i'd never
asked for
    a love that stains my fingers to the touch and it stays with me

    forevermore

i wish **to blossom** in the spring as a bright-white—pure and
simple—*daisy!*

i am not, however, because my stains are darker than dark; richer
than rich in its shade of raven feathers
i am not, however, because my impatient petals pluck before
they're ever pulled off; wished upon
i am not, however, because my being is too complicated to match
its regular counterpart
    no, no—i am not a daisy.
    but i want to be

why

if you're leaving—
answer this:
why him?
why not me? was it something i said?
something i did? something in the way i spoke?
what was it that drove you to him
instead of me
when all you ever talked about
were the fantasies our future told?
all i wanted to know was
why wasn't i the one for you?
why is that such a hard question
for you
to answer?
why?

idk

here's the thing:

you weren't like the others.

you didn't treat me like shit,
you didn't ask for anything, but time
you didn't lie to me, say "*ily, wanna meet up?*"
you didn't stroke my ego like the dick it's become
you didn't ghost me on the regular

nah, you were one of the best.

you gave me laughter, when all i wanted was to cry
you gave me a sultry, sun kissed glow on a cloudy day
you gave me an ear to listen when all other shops were
       closed
you gave me a shoulder to lean on when shit hit the fan
you gave me your opinions, rather than your directions
you gave me the truest form of you, no bullshit—just *you*
       and me

but...
i feel weird 'bout it all.
this feeling is too foreign to feel.
usually i go for the dude who's
not in to me as i am to him—
slowly becoming the norm.
i just...
idk,
you're great.
i'm not.

and *i'll love you*, i yelled,
as you drove off in the distance,
forever.

-    *nevertheless, i loved you*

valentine's day

roses are red
violets are blue
        love's givin up on me,
        so i'm givin up on you

fear + loneliness

i hate that you made me feel so alone
i'm not supposed to say this, and trust me,
i hate that i'm saying—and thinking—it, but
i'm nothing without you
and your absence scares me
because i don't know who i am without you

-   *broken china*

sharp those claws

Young huntsman stops, alone, he resides—
too deep within a forest filled of monsters—
beasts that prey on men who fear that is unknown.
His gun he grabs; young huntsman shoots into the dark—
bullet hits a creature none wish to see—
screams, the beast it does: "He who shoots, he will die!"
Scampers off, young huntsman he, into the night, away he
  goes—
the path it narrows, tricking young huntsman to his death.
Sharp those claws of ravenous beast, break the skin of that
  who slain,
blood it shoots on the path—now it's stained a hue that's
  rich with red—

fear takes many forms,
but my fear of losing you
trumps even the biggest—hairiest
of spiders crawling across my chest

- *night crawler*

up @ night

it's black, and
all is dank-dark quiet.
no one else is awake,
so i am all alone—
no one to snap to heal
these oozing wounds

memories keep me wide awake
of how happy i was with you
of how happy i was when you
were the one
keeping me up at night
with your sleepy snaps
and sweet lullaby pick-up lines

now, the only thing keeping me
up at night
is a heart that won't stop weeping
at your pictures i told
everyone i deleted
but couldn't bring myself to do

creepy creature circling its prey

Whose woods we wander through it all
never thinking but of Death—
loose leaves fill up the lane
and crumple 'neath our breath—

Out 'nd far is what we see
a creepy critter, teeth it shows—
knees wobble, it woes— "RUN!"
our senses scream, off before it knows.

Late we are—too that at much—
vexes our fears, it does that well—
quickened—lively and whip—our pace it is.
Sweat drips down our brows—so sour we smell.

In our ear, a sound so sincere—
booms so loud—quake the ground it does—
a beastly snare to which we hear.
Got us, it did, our flesh it loves—

owl eyes

at the stroke of half-past
        midnight,
                in the thicket across the garden,
                        a brawny owl sat watch.

he sat there on the branch
        until morning
                bled
                        across the sky.

golden yellow eyes,
        so, so wise—
                they creeped around
                        every corner,
                                no corner left unturned.

like a stutter, he persisted—
        coming back,
                same spot,
                        he watched the villagers

who were left defenseless
        at the hour
                which only
                        those yellow golden eyes
                                were aware and well alert.

screaming in the dark
sweating through pajamas
shifting under heavy blankets

- *nightmares*

damn the dreamer

The tower where locked she was many ago rests within
a forest so dark minds get lost in the mess
that is a terror only found at its core.
Spread throughout its darkened paths can be found
monstrous creatures who stalk their prey so well—
screams of those that perish fill the air so murky,
chills bubble on her skin—so she sits up in the sky—
forever, she waits for her prince to dodge the beasts that
        kill,
to restore her long forgotten faith that is she dreams—

"and as the casket closed—
I knew it then,
alone, I'll be—
forever"

-   *said the widow*

Evil Crow

Evil Crow—
steals my Child's food at night.
Takes it all away,
leaving my Child with none.

I despise that Crow—
that who ruined my Child's appetite.
He pecked at my Child's peace of mind,
disrupting my Child's playful pipper.

It raged—
on and on, that Wretched Crow.
It did unspeakable things that spooked my Child's slumber.
On the window sill at night, he scratched so sinister.

Evil Crow—
I grabbed my blaster—
and shot, I did, into that Evil Crow's eyes.
Then watched as the life drained from its Evil Crow eyes.

the sky cries and curses,
crackles and cackles
all night long.

i sit up in bed,
sweating trepidation.

i turn
but it's then that
i remember that
you're gone.

all of the shadows
in my room
creep around like a demon from Tartarus
that adds to and feeds
off my fear
of being
completely

alone.

- *being alone makes me feel fragile,*
  fragility scares me

I cry and scream and kick and flail my arms around the air, hoping I scare him off—it doesn't—I run and yell for help—no one answers—my knees are weak, I want to fall and give up and just lay here on the cement so he can just take me to do his bidding—

-   *self-protection*

"Pull the trigger, I dare you!
You can't do it—you *won't* do it!"

-   *said the shotgun to the head*

heartbeat slows
blood pools at the open wound
pulse fades with the passing of the light

\-   *Death takes its victim*

beating heart

my chest, it pounds against the quiet atmosphere
loudly, sounds shoot across the room
nervously, my nails i bite off habitually
take me, take me now, i tell want to scream in to the void
      of nothing, of darkness, of emptiness,

but don't—
instead, my heart
beats out of my
chest and bleeds
on the cracked floorboards

drip drip drip

peace + bliss

sunflower

happy
when all skies are gray;
and,
when i'm drenched in the b l u e s,
your y e l l o w smile
takes, takes it all
away.

hummingbird heartbeat

Flitter
Flitter

Fast flurrying of frail wings flittering by my eye

Flitter
Flitter

Happy Hummingbird, your heartbeat—
so gentle, so subtle in my ears—
so precious I could cry all my life

Flitter
Flitter

Holy Hummingbird, your wings—
how they flutter and flicker in the sunlight—
I'm in complete awe; breaking my stare would be that of a crime—

Flitter
Flitter

I die inside by the breeze your departure leaves behind
        it tickles my cheek ever so gently, the wind,
        it smells as if lavender's lips opened up and blew me
        a kiss.

Hummingbird, your heartbeat so limp and dear,
puts me fast asleep.

happier now

it took months and months and *months* of self-realization and motivation, but i'm at a place where i don't hate everything about myself. no, i'm at a place where it doesn't hurt to breathe. nope, i've move passed that feeling of wanting to vomit just to seek attention. i don't cry at night because it helps, i cry at night because i'm so fucking happy today and i fucking *love* the person i am today. i am so proud of where i'm at, i cry just thinking of the journey i went through under everyone else's radar. i fucking did it. and i'm sorry that i'm no longer sorry, i wish and hope and pray that everyone gets to this point in their lives because, honestly, i'm so uplifted—and surviving—no, not just surviving, i'm *thriving*. just look at me: my smile is finally authentic, i don't wear sweatshirt after sweatshirt to had the body i've spent so many eras hating and hiding, and i think less of how i'm seen through society's lens and only focus on what makes me smile and what makes me feel confident in my skin because for the first time in a long time, i am at peace with myself.

tickles amid my inner elbow
send tingles down my legs
to my toes they travel

-    *your touch*

shut your pretty face and dance with me

the night's still young,
put down your phone
and join me on the dance floor
of life,
where we leave our worries
behind and shake our asses like a shake weight.

words spew out of your mouth
like a broken faucet,
continuous and senseless—
wasteful, boy better blow
off all that steam from the work week

take my hand, teach me the tango,
show me your carlton,
baby, whip and nae nae if you wanna—
just shut your pretty face and
come dance the night away
with me.

m o o n l i g h t

all is calm in the world at night
above us all it shines so bright
cool air sucks hickies on my neck
oh, the moon—a lonely speck
in the sky, she enchants all with her song—
such a sight we've missed all day long

bonsai tree

the morning has always been my favorite, even though i often cheat on its beauty with the elegance of well-rested sleep. there's something refreshing about waking up to a golden sunrise on a dew-soaked morning, everything wet and crystal clear with the watered welcome to a new day's journey. if i had my life together, my morning would look like this: i'd wake up, but not get up, at 6 a.m. and read my morning meditations to motivate me through each day. after i find my zen, i'd stretch my stressed muscles and release any tension i hold onto unnecessarily. journal. i'd then journal everything. i'd push myself to let it out before i tense up because knowing me, it's bound to happen throughout the day. a wild wish of mine is a bonsai tree to cut during these early moments of the day. there's something so soothing and sensual about cutting and shaping its leaves. a part of me releases any frustrations by physically cutting something other than myself.

i've changed
i've evolved;
now,
everything i do,
i do for me.

-   *do the things that bring you bliss*

when i'm near you,
close to you,
and against you,
my knees shake.
when i hear your voice,
your pulse,
and your laughter;
how it fills the space
between us now,
it tranquilizes my rowdy waters
and settles my seas to a glass-like gleam.

-    *comforting grace*

d yellow
...ie through my broken blinds
waking me from slumber, warm with welcome

- *sunrise*

a 'restful night

Softer than a baby's blanket,
clean as a crystal whistle.

Peaceful, peaceful sky,
colored in heavenly patches of fluffy freedom.

Sharp, crisp air of a wide ocean breeze
pacifies his nose with salt.

Taste buds dance on a clean mint julep,
wild as a rebellious teenage daughter.

Mama whispers sugary lullabies,
sweet—sweet like Southern tea.

The soothing almost buzzing eases
to please the desired slumber.

Harmony, simple harmony
more serene than the morning rise,

a beloved mother's eyes
telling her sweet young prince,

a restful 'night.

five more minutes

it's morning—
and I wake up annoyed
at the world
again.

I tell my alarm that
it needs to shut up
and let me sleep
for

five

.

.

more

.

.

.

.

minu—

i'm at peace when you're around
to ease that troubled mind of mine

-    *you're my problems and answers rolled up in one*

it's morning
it's nighttime
it's time for everything,
but never time for nothing

-    *internal clock*

pillow thoughts

eyes so heavy they close
only thinking 'bout tomorrow
fading into dreams

slow dancin wit' u

the world slows down,
        nearly stopping,

        and
when we touch, collide, dance
to the soft melody—
soft like the petals
of the first rose in spring

we blossom and pollinate
in the meadow,
like we're the only flowers
blooming in the cool, temperate air.

your hand firmly in mine
made me lose track of time,
and when we stopped
i asked if we could
do it all over again

nearly midnight

Pillows and blankets are scattered.
I quiver multiple shivers,
for I am not willing to get up—

not just yet.

Cold silkiness caresses
my extended limbs—ever so carefully.
Stretching out, I kill the buzzer,
that which impedes my slumber.
I thank last night's actions—
the breeze blows in my bedroom,
toes they curl up, eyes they revolt within;
morning air—so silky pure!
The gentle, genial breeze
settles my fiery skin
bitter. It feels pearlescent to my touch—
crisp, clean
cut, and cool—
I am collected.
I'm a bear—
who's been poked out of hibernation—
I growl and bite back
against the attitudes of man.
Pillows and blankets—
I float upon, eyes I wish were closed
as I lay upon a cloud up in the sky.
If only I could be here forever,
yet work demands
every
         second;

every
day.

bubble bath

water rises
until it caps off
the tub

soapy water
turns a bubble bath
for one

rubber ducky
floats through the foam
so gently

burning candle
fills the dim room
slowly, sensuously

eyes close
head back, I drift
into tranquility—

love + longing

nightingale

song bird, song bird—
you sing a hymn all night,
its melody puts me to sleep
and away i dream
of your love song.

song bird, song bird—
i am entranced by your rhythmic
chirping; it's everything i love about you:
gentle,
guiding,
and generous.

song bird, song bird—
you are my nightingale
and you sing the song
that traps me in love's golden cage.

i'm slightly obsessed, mostly crazed

my imagination runs wild like horses
and i picture all the things i'd do to you
in a galloping leap of faith

you're perfect and gorgeous and
courageous and sensitive and sincere
and brave and endearing and loving
and gentle and kind and witty and
all the things i'm looking for all
wrapped up in one

this thing we have is scary, though,
because once there's a possibility
for something as delicate and as real as you,
there's also a chance, a slight, slight chance
that we will fall apart before we fall together

i guess that's reason my heart hurts
and my head hangs low,
i'm so obsessed with you—
everything about you turns my smile golden—
so obsessed, that i hug onto the thought of us
working towards something bigger than real,
something ideal

i spent my nights
wishing you were here
or i was there

\-   *in your absence, i grow cold*

all those spells i cast on you
didn't do
the same as what
your smile
does to me

\-   *witchcraft is trickery*

i knew it at the pacing of my heartbeat
i knew it at the sweat in the creases of my palm
i knew it at the butterfly covered lilac bush in my stomach
i knew it at the fall to the ground,
    when you swept me off my feet.

\-   *i am in love*

four a.m.

my phone says
i'm up thinking
about you
all too late
all too early
in the night
in the day.

my heart says
i'm up obsessing
far past my
bedtime
for my own good.

my mind says
i'm up dreaming
about all of
the same things
that broke my heart
before, but i
step in and say,
this time's different.

please stay

your presence warms my winter day
and ignites a soul so frozen

our conversations keep me grounded,
so that when what you say swifts me off the earth—
i stay latched in the language i long for

i

lose

my

breath

by your

charm

and
i am falling
and you are always there to catch me—

always,

so—how could i possibly live without you?

simple, classic things

sweaty hands held too-tight together,
squeeze it, squeeze it tight.

walk your foot up and down my shin
at dinner, please, footsie fantasies come to life.

text me after you get settled at home afterwards,
had a great time, you'll have to let me go for round two.

under the stars, i want to look into your jet-blue eyes,
slip into a constellation trance, fixed upon your heavenly gaze.

i couldn't care less about stupid flowers or candies,
baby all i's wantin is you to want me too.

my heart bursts with love
like fireworks,
a dancing flame,
and rain on smooth glass

-    *caress my cheek, stupid boy*

cologne

you linger on my mind
for hours, then days
at a time

your memory clings
to me like a wet bathing suit,
skin tight

at least i have your scent
still on my clothes,
i'm in love with you,

especially your
cologne

in the moments of night where it's almost dawn

Oh, how I missed a face that is of yours!
So long it's been since I've seen your charming smile—
tell me, please dear, we won't go a time so long once more!
Faded, they did—those weeks so fast, I missed you all the while—
on my trip, I couldn't but think your mind so pure—
oh, how much I thought of thee!
Assume, I only, your heart but did only go wary—
it's really not the worry, such company is but our love!
Eyes be dry, here at last—time in our chariot we have but three
hours more to be one again. Nightfall comes oh, how on the dot—
the room it fills with a sultry moonlit glow—
and in the hour so late, our clothes are all but show—

body cavities

A fire—how brightly it burns—between us now
a glow so mighty we needn't a candle to light—
Your legs, they open—a crowd that is of one they welcome—
My palms—oh, my palms—like sap off a tree,
they sweat—
Quiver and shake—my body it does—nerves relinquish they do—
Bewitching you are—your spell I fall under—
Candles out like off of our clothes—quick, nimble—mindlessly they
go—

i play connect the dots
on your dimples
and freckles.
i play hi-o cherry-o
with your navel
and follow its path
to your woods, i adventure.

-   *board game fantasies*

hourglass sands

it spews out—
such smooth silver—it glows in my hands,
your complexion it fades, passing with the light—
the time it draws closer—
"in a flash, it'll be over!" I ease the discomfort
in your heart you feel—

it's here—
kiss, we do, of but weak it is—
miss, I will, but Death is what it is—
lonely chamber emptied out of sands—
the same in our hearts it molds.

nothin but trouble

Smile so cocky it comes with veins,
you strut into the room
and I can't help but fall on the floor—
stunned by your charisma.

I tell myself—*no,*
yet—here I am writing this pity poem—
I knew it from day one, I did—
you're nothing but trouble.

I called your bluff, but
your web I walked right in—
I mean, how could I say no
to a smirk so luring?

Like catnip—I was hooked
in your swagger.
I hate myself for loving you—
boy, you're nothing but trouble.

text me back before i find somebody else

the minute i hit "send,"
my heart stops
and nothing else
functions fittingly.

instantly, i can't help
but think of what's
keeping you from
hitting me back.

are you messaging
someone else? what's
the 'sitch?' what's his
name, what's *her* name?

at times like these,
i just tell myself
i'm crazy, stupid, and
in love
with everything about you.

my eyes rollin back

my toes curl, nearly snappin off, my back arches on its own will, nearly breakin down, my palms sweat and sweat, nearly sprayin you and I, my eyes my eyes my eyes, oh *yes*—my eyes roll—they're rollin back in their sockets, my eyes are rollin back at your touch your scent your stubble growin back by the minute, oh but my eyes keep rollin back and rollin back, you do things to me I didn't know my body could do—my eyes, my eyes roll back so far, I'm blinded by your Godly presence in this mortal world too damned to dream of this hot kinda love, but you make my eyes roll back and they roll back and back and back—until all is black and wet with love's firecracker— *pop!*

mornin, b

good morning, beautiful
I dreamed of you last night—
sweetheart, the memory of your kisses
brings me goosebumps
and I wish it were for the rest of my life
that my lips meet yours
you're my north star—
guiding me to true love's kiss
without you, I'd be stumbling through the dark
good morning, and I love you
forever—

ocean wide, ocean deep

my love can go high—high'r than many o' mount'ns,
stretch further than many o' riv'rs
my love's strong'r than a batch o' oxen
pulling hundreds o' tons all the distance
oh, my love's an army of ten thousand
battle cries, rallying through the valleys
for freedom! for justice! they plea
my love's an ocean—
some say salty—bright, bright blue,
devoid of seasick sailors,
oh, how my waters they beckon and beg 'em to cross—
my love's a raging storm
whose winds do uproot the strongest and oldest of trees
my love's a mighty, mighty mother—
loving, so sweat, yet unnervingly undefeatable, it's true!—
      at most, my love's an ocean—
      for my heart feels as though it is
      ocean wide,
      ocean deep

confidence + liberation

shut the fuck up

in hindsight, i could've used you
all through high school
and up 'til now;
seriously, you would've prevented
headache, heartache— a break or two

it's fine, i'm fine now
don't sweat it
i got it
i'm good
promise

and when i fall back
in my old, bad, familiar habits—
i can manage on my own
i just tell myself to *shut the fuck up*
and move on with it

lessons learned

1. don't act so cool
   stay grounded
   and be true to yourself

2. walk as if
   the ground
   were icy waters

3. those around you mean you love
   take it, don't run from it

4. chase what you want
   in life so that you're happy
   forever

5. fireball whiskey
   is not a toy
   to play around with
   mindlessly

6. live for today;
   tomorrow is another day's gift

7. that boy who just sent you a snapchat?
   make him wait for you.
   you're worth the wait

8. don't spend so much time on the future
   that is disrupts your present-day

9. it will come, i promise

10. love is not a game,
    but more so
    a promise meant to keep

11. love more, hate less—
    always, always hate less

12. the key to success
    is through your heart
    and occasionally, fries

13. rejoice in yourself
    rejoice in your friends
    rejoice in your family
    give them all love
    every day

14. you're doing it right
    even though it feels wrong
    keep doing the things you've
    set your mind to

15. writing is a journey
    to be had
    on one's own,
    in one's own
    world—and word doc, you need a word doc

16. surround yourself
    in golden light
    and soak yourself
    in positivity

cryin over u

you think i'm cryin over u,
i just gotta laugh it over
cause that's far from true.
i aint cryin on anybody's shoulder; and
i can't stress this enough,
i'm so over everything about u.
from the lousy text sayin we were broken up,
through all the shit you put me through—
i'm standin taller than tall,
and goin on my own, head on my own damn shoulders,
wipin the tears to the left of it all,
even though all i wanna do is
cry over u.

throwing deuces around like confetti

i still wonder about you, though,
no doubt it's absolutely true.
you were a part of my thoughts
for the longest time—but
i needed to escape that
limbo-state-of-mind.

i couldn't help myself,
i *obsessed* over your dumbass picture
and now i see what a waste of time that really was.
the future i drew up for us
quickly came but of the past,

it's all good though,
i want someone who isn't so damn messy—
someone who *knows* what they want
and *knows* how to get it—
someone who treats ya' right.
does that sound gucci?
but for now,
i'll just cuddle Ruby.

voodoo doll

It's quite easy, really—you see,
take the dough—
shape it as so,
a needle you'll need—
poke it mercilessly
until the hurt passes—
quickly, it should leave.

i never needed you

i'll be back for you, you told me
so i waited

      anxiously
      excitedly
      on pins and needles

but the problem with love is
it lies
and things always change.

so, when we locked eyes
tonight
at a stupid party,
one i tried to ditch
twenty minutes in,
you
pretended as if i was

not the same person
you once imagined a life with

but

here's the thing:
i'm finally
over
you,
so, boy,
bye.

now that you've left me alone,
i can finally just breathe

-     *when the breath becomes the air*

forget goodbye

This is far from over, and I'm not going down
      without a fight.
I'm not taking any negativity, no—no I will not frown,
      even the overabundance, despite.
This isn't over, I'm not giving up on myself,
      not just like that.
I can't continue to indulge in such fantasies, farewell
      to those that ground my inner acrobat.
This isn't over, no—it can't be for I haven't said so,
      not without a chance to give.
No, it isn't over. I haven't reached the top, nor stretched my torso
      to taste the ripest fruit that the tree provides—

the daisy that never bloomed

told from day one that it needed to, one day, sprout and blossom into the beautiful, symbolistic flower that stood for purity, for innocence, for new beginnings, for beauty—the pressure of fitting in with those around it, made it keep its beauty for itself in the end.

~~i need you~~
i don't need you to validate me
i don't need you to validate me
i don't need you to validate me
i don't need you ~~to validate me~~

-    *said the boy who learned he's going*
     to be just fine on his own

on my own

somewhere along the way,
i picked up that i *needed* you
to feel like i was someone.

can't help but laugh,
because i've
learned to love
myself more than i'd ever
be able to love you.

so, news flash—
i'm 'iight and
don't need you
to light it up for me
anymore, i'm doin
so fuckin well all
on my own, but thanks
for offering to destroy
the person i love
wholeheartedly:

me.

i shouldn't,
but i'm going to
fuck you up,
fuck you over

-    *revenge*

you come back to bite
me harder than before and
i just want to scream

-     *you're my karma*
      (a haiku for you)

coming together piece by piece

it's often easier for me to point out the problem, rather than work to solve it. i want to say that it's just laziness, but i know that it's so much more than something as stand-offish as the like. i want to tell myself the truth, the real reason why i shut down, lock up, and stand still— but don't. i'm afraid of myself, in a way, i suppose that's why, but still i think there's something twice as deep and evermore. something that will take time to address, something that will take time to blossom with age. i know now that i am too bit of wingless bird to do what is i must—*fly off* towards the sunset, into the abyss of life. like a puzzle, i'm coming together to a cross-stitch of the person i'd seen so long before i set my sights on the foreseen.

ignore everything
on social media,

you're fucking *perfect*—
        as is.

- *self-confidence*

long live—
      the dancers, those that dared to dance at mid-
      night.

long live—
      this feeling, an electric blue high that runs thr-
      ough our legs

long live—
      our numbers, may all but none fall too early i-
      nto the pit of life

long live—
      these songs, those that sing even throughout t-
      he deafening quiet

and *long live*—
      our kindled spirits, our smiles that we pray st-
      and the savage monsters of Time

this moment—
      long live, this moment!

an emotional
kaleidoscope

White—
> my skin shines sparkling in the sun's sizzling streams
> of light—
Yellow—
> my smile, saturated in happiness, it shows a pride
for
> you, yellow, are such a sight to be seen!
Orange—
> endlessly summer solstice and sticky slurpees
spilling
> into my sweaty palm—
Green—
> thistles that tickle—and *poke!*—the pads of my feet
> as I trample through the tapered turf—
Purple—
> blackberry, blackberry—oh how your juices drip
> down my mouth and stain my shorts—
Navy Blue—
> midnight: so so dark, up in the sky your stars shine
> bright—my oh my, my favorite sight—
Black—
> drifting, drifting—my eyes be heavy as the
> impalpable night sky stains all of which I lie—

we arrived last monday,
and the moment we stepped
into the foggy, heavy air,
our tour guide warned us,
"watch your step out here,"
he said with guidance spritzed with humor,
"you're in the jungle now—
the thick of it all."
vines like snakes slung down,
blending in with the real ones.
bugs swarmed around us, the more
we swatted them, the deeper they pervaded
our privacy. some stang us with their stingers,
others sank their teeth in our flesh,
which left radical reddish marks for storytelling.
we were in it together, we all thought to ourselves.

our fears, though, we drowned by the rainfall each day.
rain and rain, it did. we couldn't see out too far,
the water blurred our vision. we were blinded in a new,
unfamiliar territory,
but we made it out alive to tell our friends the journey.

All my life, I've noticed that we classify;
from ideas to inanimate objects,
we objectify
its worth in our lives.
It might be a battle between:
black or white,
yes or no,
day or night
stay or go.
We have the power to turn it,
flip it,
make the switch—
believe there's more.
With our kaleidoscope, we can choose to see:
perception,
luck, and
circumstance.
So whether it's day or night,
choose to simply admit
there's a time to be right
in the heart of the abyss—
savor it.

i look through the many panes
to see a world i wished i lived in
one of colors and reflections and hues
so fluorescent and bright and pleasant
to my wondering eye.
my dreams fill up with fantasies i dare to desire
i'm pissed that i'm not there
i'm hurt that it didn't invite me to come over to stay
forever
i'm content with looking, but like a kid—I want to touch, to
feel
i look through the many panes
to see a world i see i am living now.

-    *phantasmagoria*

reflective rainbow

I see failure in the misty reflection
you tell me to look closer—
upon first glance—nothing
then—
I see it, shining and shimmering
in the light of the glimmering hues;
so many colors to watch reflect
I see that I didn't fail after all, but—
prove that I'm still fighting for an answer

up wild and free in the gorgeous, sultry dark night sky;
all the while, she conquers and makes her flight.
morning comes the hour so soon, when we have to make
        the hardest goodbye.
she provides the warmest embrace, for which i rest in the
        eye of each night.
people always ask me about the moon etched into the
thin-thin
        skin of my wrist—
dreams, i say in short. *dreams* push us through it all.
dreams, i point out, are far too important to simply be
        pushed aside and casually dismissed.
bring them in, nurture and support them; they'll treat you
        well in the long-haul.
think 'bout it: nothing, but *dreams*, force you to act for

    you

    and for you

    alone,

they give you a rich feeling that you did it all—hatched the
dream, tended to it, and laid it—all on your own.

we are a confetti-filled atmosphere,
we are the noise that bursts their eardrums,
we are a fierce too strong to be reckoned with
we are lightness
we are darkness
we are golden, sun-kissed raindrops falling from the sky
we are capable of the incapable
we are fearless when the coward took their seats
we are the resistance that the government dreads
we are the glittering fireworks that rupture the night
atmosphere
we are silver and gold in a world of neutrals
we are running toward our futures and we are
          unstoppable.

kaleidoscope

With this, too, I see

                a life that I, too, can reach.

Inside, I hide

                    a feeling

that creeps

                and lies around.

A demoralized demon,

          perpetually preying down deep

where my

              ugliness hides, that where

I hate the person

                  I once was.

For long as time, I felt confined

        to my limitations (and imitations).

              With this, now, I see

a life that I, too, deserve.

          One I won't shatter nor feel

as though I shouldn't have, but

       simply, live amongst the kaleidoscope

of refracted lights of color

                for I do

      DESERVE

this life.

     We *each* deserve

        a life to enjoy the brightest of

colors and loudest of hues,

never feeling that dubbing doubt

creep beneath the prisms

in your kaleidoscope.

swirling for solitude
changing for curious minds
transitioning for the truth
rotating for reality
playing with positivity
quickly cut from view
altered state of mind
crazed, yet craved

- *emotions*

Don't feel ashamed by the pink of your cheeks
after the snappy bitter wind bites.
Don't hide the glowing embers of your eyes—
bold, beautiful brown eyes that flash against the white
of your skin. Why a sweater so blue?
It's saddened and dull.
Don't disguise that smile, it's pure and golden!
With you around, my heart skips and lulls—
A gradient of great hues that go unspoken—
there's joy and there's sorrow.
Your fears, how they devour
today and your tomorrow,
your wisdom, colored after winter's silver bells,
oh, how you continue to thrive
by embracing each color
that tells us we're each alive—

-    *watercolor palette filled with our emotions*

i've cracked the code
to the journey towards positivity:
acknowledgement.

to feel the high,
first you have to
dive, face first,
in the low

to reap the benefits
of the sweet,
you have to taste the sour

to love,
hearts must go through a
bad break—
just once to show yourself
what it looks like to experience
something special,
something worthy of your time
that's what mastery looks, feels like

my biggest critic has always and a day been myself, and probably always will be. i tear into everything with a heavy hand for perfection, ripping the ugly to shreds. i burn through the trash quicker than swallowing the compliments they give me. i tell myself that i won't ever be "good enough" to catch my dreams, that i will only fail and fail and continue to fail. i push and push and push to be better at those few things i care so much about because my greatest fear makes them walk the line—if i fail, how can i achieve what i've worked so hard for so long for? to escape these reckless, abusive thoughts, i run to my oasis, my sanctuary, my fortress of solitude, my physical heart: my journal. i pick up a blue-ink pen and write it all out, pour it all out on the pages. my pages, stained with ink; my cheeks, stained with tears—at least, i'm shaping up just okay and working towards to positivity. i write everything as is as is as is as is and it hurts to write, but eases my sense of being, living, thinking, breathing—it all comes back once i set my pen down and close the binding of my journal.

we are fragments of broken pieces
crafted by emotions colored in each hue;
alter your stance slightly, though,
and we are reborn anew

-    *we are really just an emotional kaleidoscope*

acknowledgements

Firstly, thank you Robin Vuchnich for the GORGEOUS cover! You were so wonderful to work with for the cover art. I appreciate your attention to detail, genuine interest in my book, and the time that you put into crafting this masterpiece. I wouldn't want it any other way for my first published work. Thank you!

Secondly, thank you to anyone who was the muse for any of the pieces in this collection. Whether you broke my heart or helped mend the broken pieces, I appreciate the inspiration you ignited inside of me. Here's to you, you know who you are!

This is going to be a total cliché, but it's 100% authentic, I PROMISE—thank you to Mom, Dad, Andrew (I guess, *wink*), and Ruby and Toby (woof) for supporting everything I do and continue to do. I love you, even when I stupidly say I hate you at times. I really do love you and appreciate everything you do for me. Thank you.

Next, thank you to every one of my friends who would read my work and tell me I'm on the right track. Specifically, thank you Karlee for always telling I'm talented and doing everything right when I feel like I'm doing it wrong. You were the first to ever see any of these poems, thank you for reading them—and most importantly, thank you for not only believing in my poems, but in me. I love you, forever and always, friend.

To all of my teachers who've made an impact on my life, thank you—I DID IT!!! Specifically, thank you Corinne Biswell, Barbara Lawhorn, Christy Wherley, and Magdelyn Helwig for everything you have done and continue to do for me.

Corky, I have so many words I want to tell you to compose my thanks, but I would run this collection a thousand pages. Thank you for believing in me from day one and thank you for continuing to believe in me. I'm so thankful to call you a mentor and eventual peer. Thank you.

Barb, oh sweet, sweet Barb. Thank you for encouraging me to write and write and write and publish it all. Thank you for reading everything I ever asked for you to read. For your feedback, I thank you. Without your support or feedback, I wouldn't be the confident writer I am today; this collection certainly wouldn't be published without your passionate heart. Thank you for agreeing to write the forward for this collection without first asking what it was about or to see any of it. Your trust and faith in me pushes me forward every day. Thank you, a thousand and a million times. Thank you.

Christy, you are phenomenal. Thank you for always welcoming me into your office and for always offering your ear to anything question I had. You push me to be a better teacher each day and I can't for the day when we're peers—

and bonus points if we end up teaching at the same school! Thank you for always supporting my dreams and wishes. Truly, I appreciate everything you've done and continue to do for me.

And Magdelyn, I'm so thankful you taught ENG 200 in the fall of 2018. You introduced me to the magical world of poetry! To be honest, I came into it not really interested in poetry, but you showed us ENG 200 students the ropes and reels to poetry. It's without a doubt that I say this book wouldn't published without your authentic teaching style and genuine devotion. Thank you for introducing me to poetry and all of its glory. Thank you, you are one of the best professors at Western!

Last, but certainly not least, thank you to *you*—the reader. Thank you so much for picking up this collection. I poured my heart, body, and soul into this collection. I truly appreciate you giving my poetry your time. Thank you. From the bottom of my heart, I thank you.

sincerely,

Connor

about the author

Connor Sullivan, who writes and publishes under the name c.m. sullivan, enjoys everything about books—writing, reading, and talking about them. Those who know Connor personally can attest that his main dream has always been becoming a teacher; however, his second—less publicly known—dream has been to publish a book of his own. *an emotional kaleidoscope* makes Connor's dream come true by being his first published work. Connor lives in west-central Illinois, where he is currently working towards a Bachelor of Science in Education degree in Middle Level Education with triple endorsements in Language Arts, General Science, and Social Studies, as well as a minor in English at Western Illinois University. When Connor isn't writing, he can be found reading, snuggling his dogs, Ruby and Toby, pretending he can sing, or ordering an ungodly amount of Taco Bell at an ungodly hour of night.

CPSIA information can be obtained
at www.ICGtesting.com
Printed in the USA
LVHW112318110319
610317LV00001B/73/P